The Shape of Light

The Shape of Light

JAMES WRIGHT

Introduction by Anne Wright
Afterword by Christopher Merrill
Drawings by Joan Root

WHITE PINE PRESS / BUFFALO, NEW YORK

Publication of this book was made possible, in part, by grant from the
National Endowment for the Arts, which believes that a great nation
deserves great art, and with public funds from the New York State
Council on the Arts, a State Agency.

Printed and bound in the United States of America.

First Edition

13-digit ISBN: 978-1-893996-85-4
10-digit ISBN: 1-893996-85-9

Library of Congress Control Number: 2007921244

Published by
White Pine Press
P.O. Box 236
Buffalo, New York 14201
www.whitepine.org

Contents

Introduction

The first edition of *The Shape of Light,* a combination of James Wright's prose pieces from two previous chapbooks, *Moments of the Italian Summer* and *The Summers of James and Annie Wright,* was a delight. Now Dennis Maloney of White Pine Press has delighted me further with a new edition of this book that includes additional pieces from *This Journey.*

James began to write prose pieces (a term he preferred to prose poems) in the summer of 1973. This new form blossomed during the long, tranquil days of a sabbatical leave. We spent most of that trip in Italy and, among other places, visited Lake Garda and Verona, both of which were new to James.

Each day we would stop to sit under an umbrella at our favorite cafe by the Sirmione boat dock or under the awning of the Caffè Dante in Verona. James would take out the small notebook he used as a journal and jot down a daily entry. He also spent hours of quiet work at whatever desk or table was on hand in our various hotel rooms.

In one entry he wrote:

> All I need at bottom is a small uncluttered place
> and of course a little pasta, and a little sleep and
> the security of the people I care about.

He noted, "The way to proceed is to note as many details as I can, as they come back." The noted details included such things as a turtle, many lizards and spiders, olive blossoms, trees and rocks, events and people from his childhood in Martins Ferry, Ohio, and always the light. In 1976 Dryad Press published these first prose pieces in *Moments of the Italian Summer.*

In August of 1979, at the end of another long leave, we rented the Higgins's apartment in Paris. It was one we'd stayed in before and was a lovely place with a study for James, a big terrace, and the rue Daguerre street market just one block away. James established a daily ritual in which he got up early each morning to spend several hours with his notebook. In a letter to Leslie Marmon Silko, he wrote about the growing number of poems and prose pieces in his journal and how he copied them into a large notebook where "they will have to lie there by themselves for a while until they change. They almost always do. A poem is a very odd duck. It goes through changes—in form and color—when you leave it alone patiently, just as surely as a plant does, or an animal, or any other creature...

"Well, this new work of mine will change in time. Some of it is naturally ripening already."

When we returned from the last journey James kept the early morning routine he had established in Paris. He continued to work on the new pieces in his journal and slowly moved them into a large, black spring binder. Some of the new pieces now took place in France as well as in Italy, and one, "The Fox at Eype," in England.

James and I worked together on plans for a chapbook that would combine some of his new prose pieces with a few of mine. The rest of this recent work went in the manuscript of what was to be *This Journey*. Both books were published posthumously. Sheep Meadow Press put out the chapbook entitled *The Summers of James and Annie Wright* in 1981 and Random House followed with *This Journey* in 1982. *The Shape of Light* came in 1986, and now we have a new edition.

In these prose pieces it might seem to always be summer: summer where blissful afternoons were spent in Italy or France under clear, blue skies and brilliant sunlight, interrupted only by a gentle breeze or the sound of water. But there is a haunting undercurrent of pain or trouble in some of the work, such as the violent ugliness in "Bari, Old and Young," or the threat of aging and a tragic remembrance of World War I found in "The Sunlight Falling at Peace in Moret-sur-Loing." The focus of "The Cross" is on the brief season of life but James, in the market square of Padua, viewed …"the fruits of the season in a glory that will not last too long.

But they will last long enough"—long enough anyway, for this poet who chose to "live my life rather than not live it."

Anne Wright
New York City
December 2006

The Shape of Light

Under the Canals

Venice is a deep city, yet filmy and fragile at times. I don't mean merely its physical appearance, although the outline of roofs and towers in the early morning light can be a light and spidery thing, and the shadows among the few passages and stone streets after dark can assume almost the solidity of stone. I mean that the city can change its character, its appearance and mood, at any given moment, even in broad daylight. Consequently, it is very easy to get lost here.

Yet all one needs to do is follow the sound of water, and the things and persons of the water, to find one's way home again, wherever home may be.

We saw a very old man appear suddenly around a corner. He entered the square very slowly, for all his quick appearance, an apparition of a kind. He carried a middle-sized wooden ladder on his shoulder, and a small curious net in one hand. A chimney sweep, Annie said. Perhaps he was. With his coat elbows and his crushed hat scuffled enough, he could have prowled his way up and down the insides of these silvery, rotten walls.

But I am sure I noticed the green moon-slime on his shoes, and, until I hear otherwise, I will half-believe that he had just climbed up some of those odd stairs out of a nearby narrow canal. How can I know what he was doing under water? I can't forget it. But he was doing something. This, after all, is Venice; the very streets of the city are water; and what mag-

nificent and unseemly things must sway underneath its roads; a lost Madonna and Child frantically flung away by a harried thief last year; the perfect skeleton of a haughty cat, his bone-tail curled around his ribs and crusted with salt three centuries ago; the right hand of a disloyal artisan in spun glass, the blood long gone back to the sea; some reflection of the moon caught and kept there, snaggled between the teeth of a Turkish sailor; or the sailor himself, headless, a scimitar in one hand and a Coca-Cola in the other; a snide note from Byron; an empty American Express folder; even a chimney, swept free, till this hour passes, of all the webs they weave so stoutly down there, the dark green spiders under the water who have more than all the time they need.

There he was: a chimney sweep in warm summer weather? Hardly. A sweeper of sea-stairs.

(Venice)

The City of Evenings

The word evening has always seemed beautiful to me, and surely Venice is the city of evenings. It is renowned everywhere for its dawns, when the cathedrals and basilicas take solid shape out of the milky pearl. But their solidity is stone, even the finest of stone, the delicate sea-washed rippled marble floated here from Constantinople. It is only the evenings that give the city the shape of light; they make the darkness frail and they give substance to the light.

It is still too early for evening, and the smoke of early September is gathering on the waves of the Giudecca Canal outside my room. Steamers, motorboats, trash-scows are moving past in large numbers, and gondolas are going home. In a little while we too will meet the twilight and move through it on a vaporetto toward the Lido, the seaward island with its long beach and its immense hotel, its memories of Aschenbach and his harrowing vison of perfection, of Byron on horseback in the moonlight, and the muted shadows of old Venetians drifting as silently as possible in flight from the barbarians, drifting as far away as the island of Torcello, taking refuge as Ruskin said like the Israelites of old, a refuge from the sword in the paths of the sea. Maybe Torcello was nothing much for the princess of the sea to find, but the old Venetians discovered the true shape of evening, and now it is almost evening.

(Venice)

The Lambs on the Boulder

I hear that the Comune di Padova has an exhibition of masterpieces from Giotto to Mantegna. Giotto is the master of angels, and Mantegna is the master of the dead Christ, one of the few human beings who seems to have understood that Christ did indeed come down from the cross after all, in response to the famous jeering invitation, and that the Christ who came down was a cadaver. Mantegna's dead Christ looks exactly like a skid road bum fished by the cops out of the Mississippi in autumn just before daylight and hurried off in a tarpaulin-shrouded garbage truck and deposited in another tangle of suicides and befuddled drunkards at the rear entrance to the University of Minnesota medical school. Eternity is a vast space of distances as well as a curving infinity of time.

No doubt the exhibition in noble Padova will be a glory to behold.

But there is a littler glory that I love best. It is a story, which so intensely ought to be real that it is real.

One afternoon the mature medieval master Cimabue was taking a walk in the countryside and paused in the shade to watch a shepherd boy. The child was trying to scratch sketches of his lambs on a boulder at the edge of the field. He used nothing, for he could find nothing, but a little sharp pebble.

Cimabue took the shepherd boy home with him and gave him some parchment and a nail or a crayon or something or other, and began to show him how to draw and form lines into the grandeur of faces other than the sweet faces of sheep.

The shepherd boy was Giotto, and he learned how to draw and form lines into the grandeur of faces other than the sweet faces of sheep. I don't give a damn whether you believe this story or not. I do. I have seen faces of angels drawn by Giotto. If angels do not look like Giotto's angels, they have been neglecting their health behind God's back.

One of my idle wishes is to find that field where Cimabue stood in the shade and watched the boy Giotto scratching his stone with his pebble.

I would not be so foolish as to prefer the faces of the boy's lambs to the faces of his angels. One has to act his age sooner or later.

Still, this little planet of rocks and grass is all we have to start with. How pretty it would be, the sweet faces of the boy Giotto's lambs gouged, with infinite and still uncertain and painful care, on the side of a boulder at the edge of a country field.

I wonder how long Cimabue stood watching before he said anything. I'll bet he watched for a very long time. He was Cimabue.

I wonder how long Giotto worked before he noticed that he was being watched. I'll bet he worked a very long time. He was Giotto.

He probably paused every so often to take a drink of water and tend to the needs of his sheep, and then returned patiently to his patient boulder, before he heard over his shoulder in the twilight the courtesy of the Italian good evening from the countryside man who stood, certainly out of the little daylight left to the shepherd and his sheep alike.

I wonder where that boulder is. I wonder if the sweet faces of the lambs are still scratched on its sunlit side.

By God I know this much. Worse men than Giotto have lived longer than Giotto lived.

And uglier things than Giotto's wobbly scratches on a coarse boulder at the edge of a grassy field are rotting and toppling into decay at this very moment. By the time I reach Padova at fifteen minutes past four this afternoon, I wouldn't be a bit surprised to hear that Rockefeller's Mall in Albany, New York, had begun to sag and ooze its grandiose slime all over the surrounding city of the plain, and it will stink in the nostrils of God Almighty like the incense burned and offered up as a putrid gift on the altars of the Lord, while the King Jeroboam the Second imprisoned the righteous for silver and sold the poor for the buckles on a pair of shoes.

Giotto's boyish hand scratched the sweet faces of lambs on a coarse stone.

I wonder where the stone is. I will never live to see it.

I lived to see the Mall in Albany, though.

In one of the mature Giotto's greatest glories, a huge choir of his unutterably beautiful angels are lifting their faces and are becoming the sons of the morning, singing out of pure happiness the praises of God.

Far back in the angelic choir, a slightly smaller angel has folded his wings. He has turned slightly away from the light and lifted his hands. You cannot even see his face. I don't know why he is weeping. But I love him best.

I think he must be wondering how long it will take Giotto to remember him, give him a drink of water, and take him back home to the fold before it gets dark and shepherd and sheep alike lose their way in the darkness of the countryside.

(Padua)

21

The Fruits of the Season

It is a fresh morning of late August in Padova. After the night's rain, the sun is emerging just enough so far to begin warming the grapes, melons, peaches, nectarines, and the other fruits that will soon fill this vast square. Women and children in bright flower-print dresses are already beginning to amble from stall to stall.

At the very far end of the square I can see the azure and golden face of the town clock on the Torre dell'Orologio.

A baker with white flour sprinkled all over his boots just drifted across the extreme right corner of my eye.

It is all commonplace, ordinary, the firm shaping of the morning in an Italian city of middling size.

And yet—to my left I can see the entire front length of the Palazzo della Ragione, on whose second floor the community has arranged a huge exhibit of paintings, the enduring fruits of five hundred years.

And spread below the faces of those peculiarly tender and fierce angels, the men and women and their children are still arriving from the countryside, arranging for our slow ambling choice the heaps of grapes, melons, peaches, nectarines, and all the other fruits of the season in a glory that will not last too long.

But they will last long enough. I would rather live my life than not live it. The grapes in a smallish stall are as huge and

purple as smoke. I have just eaten one. I have eaten the first
fruit of the season, and I am in love.

(Padua)

A Small Grove

Outside our window we have a small willow, and a little beyond it a fig tree, and then a stone shed. Beyond the stone the separate trees suddenly become a grove: a lemon, a mimosa, an oleander, a pine, one of the tall slender cypresses that a poet here once called candles of darkness that ought to be put out in winter, another willow, and a pine.

She stands among them in her flowered green clothes. Her skin is darker gold than the olives in the morning sun. Two hours ago we got up and bathed in the lake. It was like swimming in a vein. Everything that can blossom is blossoming around her now. She is the eye of the grove, the eye of mimosa and willow. The cypress behind her catches fire.

(Torri del Benaco)

Flowering Olives

It is futile to pretend I am looking at something else. In fact, I am doing my best to gaze as deeply as I can into the crevice of a single olive blossom. There must be hundreds of thousands of these tiny flowers, falling all over themselves among the silver leaves of a single small tree. Too many for one tree to bear, they gather in heaps beneath the twisted branches, clusters so thick on the top of the low stone wall, all the breeze can do is blow them back and forth across each other, the way a larger wind can do no more with sand than allow it to build and dissolve and rebuild itself into dunes. I have a single olive flower in my palm. I mean I had one. Now the breeze has it, and I will never catch another. The whole mile of this mountain road high above tiny golden Gargnano gleams right now in a momentary noon of olive flowers, and I am the only darkness alive in the Alps.

The Legions of Caesar

Today, on the Feast of the Assumption, the Congress of the United States has required the President to order a cessation of bombing in Cambodia. Three men are standing below me on the shore of Lake Garda. They poise on the rocks, trailing their fishing lines in the clear water. Now and again a man draws in his line. Each carries a clear plastic bag perhaps one-third filled with piccolini. The glittering silver creatures have been living in this water surely since Catullus was a boy. The year he was born, the legions of Julius Caesar attempted to invade Britain, and failed. The year he died, thirty years later, they tried again, and more or less succeeded. A Roman temple once stood in Britain, in Dorchester, Dorset, and now it is the site of the Church of St. Peter's and All Saints.

In front of that church this morning, far away on that northern island, cut off long ago from all other human beings while a poet grieved for his first days, the statue of William Barnes turns slowly greener as he looks down the West High Street towards the King's Arms Hotel. There, once only, there stood in the front doorway the most beautiful girl he had ever seen or was ever to see in his life. He lived a long time, and so did she. Below me on the olive-silver pebbles of the Garda shore, some small boys are scampering in search of an escaped piccolino. They are serious, hurrying, before the little fish stops struggling back towards the water and turns to stone. I don't know what time it is in Cambodia.

I wonder if there is ever any silence there. Where is it, hiding from the invaders? The sunlight once glinted off William Barnes's coffin. From a hill so far away it seemed the other side of the earth, his friend Thomas Hardy wrote down the sunlight as a signal. He knew his friend was opening a hand, saying goodbye.

(Torri del Benaco)

Piccolini

Looming and almost molten and slowly moving its gold down the hill just behind my back is the summer villa of the poet, the Grotte de Catullo.

But I care more now for the poetry of the present moment. An easy thousand of silver, almost transparent piccolini are skimming the surface of the long slab of volcanic stone. They swim through a very tiny channel at the very rim of the lake. They tickle the skin of my ankles, smaller than Latin diminutives.

Catullus, grieving over his Lesbia's sparrow, turned *misere* from harsh *wretched* into *miselle,* poor and little and lovely and gone, all in one word.

But those tiny fish that tickle the skin of my ankles are already so diminutive that they would have dissolved altogether into droplets of mist at a mere touch of Catullus's fingertip. I reckon that is why he never wrote of them by name, but left them tiny and happy in their lives in the waters, where they still have their lives and seem to enjoy tickling the skin of my ankles.

(Sirmione)

The Language of the Present Moment

Off the shore of Gargnano the mountains in this summer mist look barren. Tall and short mountains stand still beside me as I drift past on Lake Garda. They throw their own flowers on the water. It is warmer than the oldest olive.

A few miles up the lake a town called Limone long ago gave up hope of surviving. The lemons of Sicily, quicker and more numerous, banish the town I will see, back to its own shadow that lies in the Garda water like a garland.

Limone, wreath of the Garda mountains, the stone villa of Catullus still stands down at the far southern end of the lake. I hope you are in blossom when his ghost comes home.

(Gargnano)

The Gift of Change

Of all the creatures, they seem to know best the art of sunning themselves. Without brooding unhappily, they understand where the best shades are. It is next to impossible to catch them and imprison them in the usual human ways, because they live in perpetual surrender: They love to become whatever it is that gazes upon them or holds them. They can turn as precisely green as the faintest hint of moss-shadow thirty seconds after noon, or a little gray knitted into silver of drying algae buoyed up ashore and abandoned there to the random wind of children's feet in flight.

But the lizard lying beside me now has gone too far. Wholly abandoning himself to his gift of change, he lifts his head above the edge of a linden blossom freshly fallen and alone. His exquisite hands have given up clinging to anything. They lie open. The leaf on the flower is so smooth, a light wind could blow him away. I wonder if he knows. If he knows, I wonder that my breath doesn't blow him away. I am that close to him, and he that close to me. He has gone too far into the world to turn back now. His tail has become a spot on the sun, the delicate crease between his shoulder blades, the fold in a linden leaf, his tongue finer and purer than a wild hair in my nostril, his hands opener than my hands. It is too late to turn back into himself. I can't even faintly begin to understand what is happening behind his serene face, but to me he looks like the happiest creature alive in Italy.

The Secret of Light

I am sitting contented and alone in a little park near the Palazzo Scaligere in Verona, glimpsing the mists of early autumn as they shift and fade among the pines and city battlements on the hills above the river Adige.

The river has recovered from this morning's rainfall. It is now restoring to its shapely body its own secret light, a color of faintly cloudy green and pearl.

Directly in front of my bench, perhaps thirty yards away from me, there is a startling woman. Her hair is as black as the inmost secret of light in a perfectly cut diamond, a perilous black, a secret light that must have been studied for many years before the anxious and disciplined craftsman could achieve the necessary balance between courage and skill to stroke the strange stone and take the one chance he would ever have to bring that secret to light.

While I was trying to compose the preceding sentence, the woman rose from her park bench and walked away. I am afraid her secret might never come to light in my lifetime. But my lifetime is not the only one. I will never see her again. I hope she brings some other man's secret face to light, as somebody brought mine. I am startled to discover that I am not afraid. I am free to give a blessing out of my silence into that woman's black hair. I trust her to go on living. I believe in her black hair, her diamond that is still asleep. I would close my eyes to daydream about her. But those silent companions who watch over me from the insides of my eyelids are too brilliant for me to meet face to face.

The very emptiness of the park bench just in front of mine is what makes me happy. Somewhere else in Verona at just this moment, a woman is sitting or walking or standing still upright. Surely two careful and accurate hands, total strangers to me, measure the invisible idea of the secret vein in her hair. They are waiting patiently until they know what they alone can ever know: that time when her life will pause in mid-flight for a split second. The hands will touch her black hair very gently. A wind off the river Adige will flutter past her. She will turn around, smile a welcome, and place a flawless and fully formed Italian daybreak into the hands.

I don't have any idea what his face will look like. The light still hidden inside his body is no business of mine. I am happy enough to sit in this park alone now. I turn my own face toward the river Adige. A little wind flutters off the water and brushes past me and returns.

It is all right with me to know that my life is only one life. I feel like the light of the river Adige.

By this time, we are both an open secret.

(Verona)

33

Magnificence

They tell me that the Arena in Verona is the most beautifully preserved Roman amphitheatre in Italy, and I believe them. Twenty thousand people could sit in it comfortably. On a sunlit day its pink and white marble glow from within, and they glow from within when it is raining.

The Arena is magnificent. It means that it is greatly made. It must be twenty-five hundred years old. The Romans, like Octavius and Cicero, were sometimes as noble as Ortega in his intelligent anguish could hope for; and even his hopes were harsh and critically severe.

In this setting, whose grandeur consists in its uncluttered purity and simplicity of design, Verdi's *Requiem* emerged with exquisite gentleness, tenderness, and sadness. Of course, the trumpets were played high at the rim of the Arena. No human Director could have resisted that opportunity. But the great Veronese musicians were so masterful in their understanding of the music, its shapeliness as fully as its clear depth of stillness all the more passionate for its revelations of silence, that during one brief passage while orchestra, chorus, and soloists were all singing lucidly and quietly together, we heard a cricket singing in the darkness at the farthest rim of the Arena.

His song was not extraordinarily melodious. He was evening. He was not trying to compete with Verdi. I think he was just trying to sing himself to sleep among the warm darkened stones.

It was characteristic of the Veronese company that the Director of the chorus had concealed himself head and shoulders behind a discreetly colored screen behind the soloists.

Only occasionally, at some moment of absolute necessity for the evocation of the chorus, we could see his beautiful hands fluttering with perfect precision above the screen, like the wings of a happy yet teetotalling cabbage-white butterfly.

For some reason known possibly to God in His more responsive moments of attentiveness, one of the softest passages of the *Requiem* was joined from the rear end of the Arena by an extremely coarse whistle of the sort that New York delicatessen managers make when they catch small children in the act of snitching candy placed by an oversight near the entrance to the store. I do pray our cousins from Jersey go elsewhere for their vacations.

The musicians paid no attention whatever, and softly though they sang, their music rose above his cacophony, as Verdi himself, a human artist whose soul had the shape and sound of something greatly made, was present among us at once in time and beyond time, almost beyond sound, at the same moment and in the same space on one of the earth's loveliest places, both diminutive and vast, very like the city of Verona itself.

Very, very like.

(Verona)

Saying Dante Aloud

You can feel the muscles and veins rippling in widening and rising circles, like a bird in flight under your tongue.

(Verona)

The Silent Angel

As I sat down by the bus window in the gate of Verona, I looked over my left shoulder. A man was standing in one of the pink marble arches at the base of the great Roman Arena. He smiled at me, a gesture of the utmost sweetness, such as a human face can rarely manage to shine with, even a beloved face that loves you in return.

He seemed dressed like a musician, as well he might have been, emerging for a moment into the sunlight from one of the secluded and cool rehearsal chambers of the upper tiers of the Arena.

As the bus driver powered his motor and drew us slowly around the great public square, the Piazza Bra, the man in the half-golden rose shadow of the Arena kept his gaze on my face. He waved goodbye to me, his knowing eyes never leaving me as long as he could still see any of me at all, though how long that was I don't precisely know.

He raised his hand at the last moment to wave me out of Verona as kindly as he could. He held in his right hand what seemed to be a baton, and it hung suspended for a long instant in the vast petals of rose shadows cast down by the marble walls. Even after he had vanished back into the archway I could still see his baton.

Oh, I know it was not a baton. I was far away now, and all I could see behind me were the diminishing cicadas, lindens, and slim cedars rising, one feather folding upwards into another, into the spaces of evergreen and gold beyond the Roman Arena, beyond the river and the hills beyond the river, the beginning of everlasting change, Saint Martin's summer. All those trees, the durable and the momentary confused with one another into the eternity of Saint Augustine's despair of time. They will still be rising there long after even the Giusti Gardens, where Goethe walked, have run back to weeds, a few of my beloved lizards left to make company with them perhaps, a spider or two still designing for days and then patiently building the most delicate of ruins.

I could not afford to let myself think of the River Adige any longer, because I loved it too much. The wings of the smiling musician are folded. His baton, grown cool again by this time, rests on his knees. I can imagine that all the other musicians have risen into the riverside hills for the night, and my musician, who meant me no harm and only wanted to wave me away as gently as possible out of the beautiful space he guarded, is himself asleep with the late crickets along the river.

I turned at last away from the city, gritted my teeth, two of which are broken and snaggled, fingered the shred of pink marble in my jacket pocket, and forced my face toward Milano with its factories, London with its fear and hopelessness, and beyond that, the final place, New York, America, hell on earth.

I felt fallen. But not very happy. Nor lucky either.

The musician had not played me a single tune, he had not sung me a single song. He just waved me as gently as he could on the way out, the way that is my own, the lost way.

I suppose I asked for it. And he did his best, I suppose. He owns that heavenly city no more than I do. He may be fallen, as I am. But from a greater height, unless I miss my guess.

(Verona)

Two Moments in Rome

How Spring Arrives

The very last snow, gritty and cruel as the wrinkles scarred in the corners of a fanatic's mouth, has disappeared overnight. Eternal winter was merely yesterday. True, high on the Borghese cliffs these gardens are still crowded with dead branches. The gross limb of a pine, torn from the body by some blind night wind, shoulders some tiny bushes out of its way. An entire oleander, uprooted weeks ago, turns harder with decay. Slouched on a stone bench, it casts a sneering shadow. The dead loiter indecently here in the fresh sunlight, bound and determined to get revenge on somebody if it's the last thing they ever do.

Three girls are coming up the path. They are so excited they can't keep their feet still. They are not running. But they touch the ground so quickly, they scarcely touch it at all. All three shake out their black hair. One after another they take off their sweaters. At each end of the stone bench, they pluck up the dead oleander as though it weighed nothing at all, and toss it out of the way. Their liquid Italian has become one continuous stream, with birds nesting all round it.

They, too, must have slept all night with their eyes open.

REFLECTIONS

At noon on a horizon the Colosseum poises in mid-flight, a crumbling moon of gibbous gold. It catches an ancient light, and gives form to that light. Gazing at the Colosseum from a spot two miles away, I feel as though I had just caught a glimpse of a girl's face. Young and alone, she is sitting high up on the stone, glancing about for her friends. Bored, she ignores that tangle of skinny mumblers far below her in the arena. She is waiting for the entrance of the animals.

Now, beyond the Colosseum, another moon, a day moon, appears in the sky. Even its little scars are ghosts.

On Having My Pocket Picked in Rome

These hands are desperate for me to stay alive. They do not want to lose me to the crowd. They know the slightest nudge on the wrong bone will cause me to look around and cry aloud. Therefore the hands grow cool and touch me lightly, lightly and accurately as a gypsy moth laying her larvae down in that foregone place where the tree is naked. It is only when the hands are gone, I will step out of this crowd and walk down the street, dimly aware of the dark infant strangers I carry in my body. They spin their nests and live on me in their sleep.

A Lament for the Martyrs

I am sitting in an outdoor cafe across the street from the Colosseum. The noon is so brilliant that I have to wear my dark glasses. You would think a Roman noon could lay even the Colosseum wide open.

But darknesses still foul the place and its hateful grandeur. The Roman Chamber of Commerce and Betelgueze in combine could gut the Colosseum by day or by night till the ghost of Mussolini and the ghost of God turned blue in the face, and light wouldn't mean a thing in that darkness. Cities are times of day. Once Rome was noon. To take a slow lazy walk with Quintus Horatius Flaccus at four o'clock in the night was to become light. If you don't believe me, I offer you a method of scientific verification. I lay you eight to five that you will go blind if you take a walk at high noon with the President of the United States. I love my country for its light. I love Rome because Horace lived there. I am afraid of the dark. I am game to live with intelligent sinners. Sometimes these days the Romans say that whatever the Barbarians left behind was later sacked and raped by the Barberinis, the noble family who needed the remnant marble for their country palaces. I find them fair enough for me. When I was a boy, the mayors of five towns in the Ohio River Valley solved the practical problems of prohibition by picking the purest and most perfect bootlegger between Pittsburgh and Cincinnati to become Chairman of the Committee for Liquor Control.

I think it would be wicked for me to wonder what the five mayors did with their cut in private. All I know is that within a year after Milber's public appointment to a legal office, a symphony orchestra mysteriously appeared in one town, two spacious football stadiums appeared in two other towns, the madame of the cathouse in Wheeling was appointed a dollar-a-year man by the Federal Government, and I lost an essay-contest whose subject was the life and work of William Dean Howells, an American author who was born in Martins Ferry, Ohio, for Christ's sake, and whose books I had never even heard of, much less read. (As I look back over the shadows of the years, I confess that I have read one of his novels. But I like him. He was a good friend of Mark Twain.)

But right now the Roman noon is so brilliant that it hurts my eyes. I sip my cappuccino at a wobbly sidewalk table and ponder the antiquities of my childhood: the beautiful river, that black ditch of horror; and the streetcars. Where have they gone now, with their wicker seats that seemed to rattle behind the dull headlights in the slow dusk, in summer where everything in Ohio ran down and yet never quite stopped?

Now, the Romans and the discovered Americans stroll blinded in the Colosseum deaf to the shadows the place never loses, even at noon in Rome, that was for a little while one of the few noons.

Some archaeologist gouged out the smooth dust floor of

the Colosseum to make it clean. The floor now is a careful revelation. It is an intricate and intelligent series of ditches, and the sun cannot reach them. They are the shadows of starved people who did not even want to die. They were not even Jews.

There is no way to get rid of the shadows of human beings who could find God only in that last welcome of the creation, the maws of tortured animals.

Is that last best surest way to heaven the throat of the hungry? If it is, God is very beautiful, if not very bright.

Who are the hungry? What color is a hungry shadow?

Even the noon sunlight in the Colosseum is the golden shadow of a starved lion, the most beautiful of God's creatures except maybe horses.

(Rome)

The Brief Season

As we rode the train south from Florence, through the slow green castled countryside, I began to fancy that Italy had gone back to the original grass for good. The dark ilex and the luminous double-cherry rose everywhere by the rivers, and the rivers, too, rose, though here they posed no danger to any human place, for all the towns were pinnacles, more or less. Orvieto alone, set delicately at the top of four rising natural walls, seemed defenseless against flood from the river. It is no use objecting that Orvieto stands above all the rivers of the earth. The river that flows by Orvieto is not one of the rivers of the earth. The shepherds who live there have all of them long ago drowned in green light, and two of them a moment ago have risen for the brief season, to stand on the cliff and wave to us as we hurry past.

The Turtle Overnight

I remember him last twilight in his comeliness. When it began to rain, he appeared in his accustomed place and emerged from his shell as far as he could reach—feet, legs, tail, head. He seemed to enjoy the rain, the sweet-tasting rain that blew all the way across lake water to him from the mountains, the Alto Adige. It was as near as I've ever come to seeing a turtle take a pleasant bath in his natural altogether. All the legendary faces of broken old age disappeared from my mind, the thickened muscles under the chins, the nostrils brutal with hatred, the murdering eyes. He filled my mind with a sweet-tasting mountain rain, his youthfulness, his modesty as he washed himself all alone, his religious face.

For a long time now this morning, I have been sitting at this window and watching the grass below me. A moment ago there was no one there. But now his brindle shell sighs slowly up and down in the midst of the green sunlight. A black watchdog snuffles asleep just beyond him, but I trust that neither is afraid of the other. I can see him lifting his face. It is a raising of eyebrows toward the light, an almost imperceptible turning of the chin, an ancient pleasure, an eagerness.

Along his throat there are small folds, dark yellow as pollen shaken across a field of camomilla. The lines on his face suggest only a relaxation, a delicacy in the understanding of the grass, like the careful tenderness I saw once on the face of a hobo in Ohio as he waved greeting to an empty wheat field from the flatcar of a freight train.

But now the train is gone, and the turtle has left his circle of empty grass. I look a long time where he was, and I can't find a footprint in the empty grass. So much air left, so much sunlight, and still he is gone.

A Snail at Assisi

The snail shell has lain up here all summer along, I suppose. It is smaller than my thumbnail, where it rests now, but it casts its light shadow huge on the ground, and my shadow is there, following very carefully. Already the light has taken my shadow into the air and laid it down the slope below me, where it grows longer and longer, always moving, yet hardly to be seen moving. The air is dry far up here on the highest hill in Assisi, on the far side of the fortress wall where the earth falls nearly straight down. Even as I squint in the sun and try to bear it alive, I wonder how the tiny snail was alive and climbed and climbed and made it all the way up to this pinnacle, the armed building and the arrow-skewered wall. The great hollow skeleton of this fortress is empty now, its back turned away from Francis's solitary hill, its face still set grimly toward Perugia. The snail is long gone, maybe lifted high into sunlight, devoured by songbirds between one fortress and another. By this time, one more long summer afternoon is nearly over. My shadow and the shadow of the snail shell are one and the same.

A Letter to Franz Wright

Twice when I was young, I stood on the side of Fujiyama. I have drifted down the Seine in a boat while the summer rain turned gray; and, along the Seine in late twilight, I glimpsed quite adequate shadows of several rats undoubtedly descended from the fellow-fugitives of François Villon, who learned where he could learn it. At the Volksoper in Vienna I have looked down from the balcony and seen a trumpeter crouch over and hand a glass of wine to a violinist right in the middle of a performance of *Der Zigeunerbaron*. And once I spent an entire day of my life (my life!) talking with Pablo Neruda and looking into his face.

But I have never, anywhere, anytime, seen anything so appallingly beyond accounting for as a place in Tuscany in late autumn. I have come, and not for the first time, to the limits of my own language. All I have with me at this moment is the memory of a time so recent that I can't yet bear to free it to live its own life in the "just city and free land" of the past. But, come to think of it, the memory is not all I have. There are these fragments of words I picked up on the hither side of my limits. I am sending them to you, because you will love them. Consequently, you will know to piece them together into a vision of your own design. Your imagination is not mine. How could it be? Who would want it to be? I wouldn't. You wouldn't. But I love both, so I trust yours. Here are some fragments of my hammer that broke against a wall of jewels.

Darkness fell suddenly one evening as Annie and Janie and I descended from the fortress of Volterra, which still broods suspiciously over the small valleys of Tuscany. The fortress by dusk looks like a paranoid dragon or, except for the city's severe dark beauty, like Nixon keeping watch over uncurtained windows where some voluptuous young woman or man has just slipped off the National Security and stretches naked by the window before turning out the light.

We drove for a while, and even got lost, and found our way again at a tiny little bar-restaurant at the edge of a village. An almost absurdly beautiful girl greeted us, gave us some coffee and grappa, spread out a huge map of Tuscany on the table, and sped us on our way with God. We finally found the sign we needed: SAN GIMIGNANO. Then we drove up, and up, and around, and up, and around, and up again, till we found ourselves picking our way in semi-darkness. (The headlights burned out in our rented Fiat.) It was almost like being in Ohio, and I felt a momentary convulsion of homesickness.

Then we emerged on a town square, not a very large one as piazzas go, and checked in at a hotel over in the corner. The town seemed pleasant enough. We were road-weary and hungry. We stepped a few doors down the street to a trattoria for a small late meal, and went back to bed.

The next morning Annie rose first, opened the curtained

doors to bright sunlight, and went out on the balcony. I thought I heard her gasp. When she came back into the room again, she looked a little pale, and said, "I don't believe it."

San Gimignano is poised hundreds of feet in the air. The city is comparatively small, and it is perfectly formed. We felt ourselves strange in that presence, that city glittering there in the lucid Tuscan morning, like a perfectly cut little brilliant sparkling on the pinnacle of a stalagmite. Far below us we could look almost straight down into vineyards and fields where people, whole families, even small children, had evidently been at work for hours. In all directions below us were valleys whose villages were just beginning to appear out of the mist, a splinter of a church here, an olive grove there. It was a life in itself.

The wall is still standing.

(San Gimignano)

A Reply To Matthew Arnold on My Fifth Day in Fano

"In harmony with Nature? Restless fool . . .
Nature and man can never be fast friends. . . ."

It is idle to speak of five mere days in Fano, or five long days, or five years. As I prepare to leave, I seem to have just arrived. To carefully split yet another infinitive, I seem to have been here forever or longer, longer than the sea's lifetime and the lifetimes of all the creatures of the sea, than all the new churches among the hill pastures and all the old shells wandering about bodiless just off the clear shore. Briefly in harmony with nature before I die, I welcome the old curse:

a restless fool and a fast friend to Fano, I have brought this wild chive flower down from a hill pasture. I offer it to the Adriatic. I am not about to claim that the sea does not care. It has its own way of receiving seeds, and today the sea may as well have a flowering one, with a poppy to float above it, and the Venetian navy underneath. Goodbye to the living place, and all I ask it to do is stay alive.

Bari, Old and Young

The old women of Bari near the sea sit in the small shadows of open doors. Their faces are beautifully darkened in the sunlight. Their hair is gray enough. They have seen the wars. They have known the young Germans blundering and falling out of the sky like poisoned moths. The young men in Bari today swagger and smirk as though no one had ever lived before, as though no one had ever died. Forever titivating their lank hair in the Adriatic breeze, voluptuously caressing their own armpits, they love to be told they are the lost youth, unemployed and betrayed by The System. Their motorcycles whinny insanely along the dark streets, and they are interested in women only to frighten them. They are too mindless to be skillful thieves. But the old women of Bari in their open doors know that young men will find something else to do, and I walk in this city as frightened as an old sea woman startled by moths.

Once the old city of Bari rose and gathered its companions out of the sea. But the new city, a growth of our present desperate century, squats a little inland, companionless. It is no place for solitude. Already the stony faces of new tall buildings are beginning to crumble.

On my last day here, I will walk carefully through the barren places and find the past again, the old city where I can stand solitary beside the noble churches. And beyond the old city, even beyond the past, there is the sea itself, the ancient freshness of the natural world that God, stirring in His lone-liness and unapproached in His light, breathed upon. The fragrance of the water moves heavily and slowly with mussel shells and the sighs of drowned men. There is nothing so heavy with earth as the sea's breath and the breath of fresh wilderness, the camomilla fields along the shore. I would like to stand among them and breathe their air, one more day of my life, before I have to turn around and make my way back to this present century, back through the ugliness of vicious young faces who will leave no churches behind them in the fullness of their age, but only the blind scars of motorcycle tires, the wrinkles of panic on women's faces, and an echo of brutal laughter at the edge of the sea.

The Limpet in Otranto

These limpets have lain empty and bodiless for long years now. Flecks of brown gold gather on their slopes like old flowers on hills at the end of autumn. They shine, even when the sun has gone down. Virgil approached them and listened inside them. But their caves were too shallow and bright to contain any ghosts. Their bodies were already gone a long time into the air. Cloud shadows and the shadows of scarred headlands fell all over the old man's shoulders, like oak leaves, the old everlasting bronzes of November, the tragic sea-faces of the trees in North Carolina, that tremble and grow older all through the year, but never fall. Caressing the inner side of a limpet with one finger, Virgil turned back inland. The purple of thistles aristocratically brushed his knees aside. He heard a voice in a tree, crying in Greek, "Italy. Italy." He listened again to the limpet in his hand. It said nothing.

Time

Once, with a weak ankle, I tried to walk. All I could do was spin slowly a step or two, and then sit down. There has to be some balance of things that move on the earth. But this morning a small tern is flying full of his strength over the Ionian Sea. From where I stand, he seems to have only one wing. There is either something wrong with my eyes in the sunlight or something unknown to me about the shadow that hangs broken from his left shoulder. But the shadow is no good to me now. He has dropped it into the sea. There has to be some balance of things that move on the earth. But he is not moving on the earth. Both of my ankles are strong. My hair is gray.

A Mouse Taking a Nap

I look all alike to him, one blur of nervous mountains after another. I doubt if he loses any sleep in brooding and puzzling out why it is I don't like him. The huge slopes and valleys, golden as wild mustard flowers in midsummer, that he leaves lying open and naked down the sides of a Gorgonzola, seem to him only a discovery, one of the lonely paradises: nothing like the gray wound of a slag heap, nothing like the streams of copperous water that ooze out of the mine-mouths in southern Ohio. I wonder what it seems to him, his moment that he has now, alone with his own sunlight in this locked house, where all the cats are gone for a little while, hunting somebody else for a little while.

Camomilla

Summer is not yet gone, but long ago the leaves have fallen. They never appeared to gather much sunlight or threw a measurable shade, even when they were most alive. They hid as long as they could beneath the white flowers and seemed to turn their faces away. They were like the faces of frightened people in a war. They silently wish they were anonymous, but they know that sooner or later someone will find them out. Everything secret to them will become commonplace to an army of invading strangers. Every stranger will know that each native of the defeated place was given at his birth, like a burden, the names of both his parents and his grandparents and great-grandparents, until there is scarcely enough room on a police form for all the names he carries around with him. Just like such brutally ransacked people, the camomilla leaves turn their faces away. If I could look toward them long enough in this field, I think I would find them trying to hide their birthmarks and scars from me, pretending they had no beards or ribbons or long braids or half-legible letters from home hidden uselessly beneath their clothes. The faces of camomilla leaves would wish me away again, wish me back into the sea again, wish me to leave them alone in peace.

Regret for a Spider Web

Laying the foundations of community, she labors all alone. Whether or not God made a creature as deliberately green as this spider, I am not the one to say. If not, then He tossed a star of green dust into one of my lashes. A moment ago, there was no spider there. I must have been thinking about something else, maybe the twenty-mile meadows along the slopes of the far-off mountain I was trying to name, or the huge snows clinging up there in summer, with their rivulets exploding into roots of ice when the night comes down. But now all the long distances are gone. Not quite three inches from my left eyelash, the air is forming itself into avenues, back alleys, boulevards, paths, gardens, fields, and one frail towpath shimmering as it leads away into the sky.

Where is she?

I can't find her.

Oh: resting beneath my thumbnail, pausing, wondering how long she can make use of me, how long I will have sense enough to hold still.

She will never know or care how sorry I am that my lungs are not huge magnificent frozen snows, and that my fingers are not firmly rooted in earth like the tall cypresses. But I have been holding my breath now for one minute and sixteen seconds. I wish I could tower beside her forever, and be one mountain she can depend upon. But my lungs have their own cities to build. I have to move, or die.

In Memory of the Ottomans

This man, mending his nets as the sun goes down, tells me religiously something I find dark: fog in the countryside of Otranto is unknown. As the starfish in the evening condense deep in the water, the light does not know what to do with itself. So the brown ridges down one side of the man's face turn green as spring rocks. Fog is unknown in Otranto, offshore from Otranto, behind Otranto. I can't believe he has never gone there. He won't say anything more about it, land or sea. What language do the hawks' tongues cry in for prayer, in that wilderness where the sea loses its way? I find this man dark. We both peer toward Greece, toward the horizon. The moon sways like a blunted scimitar.

In Gallipoli

Gray as the sea moss wavering among the green shallows along the shore, her hair blows shaggy. The sky holds. She lifts a cluster of grapes, aloof and strangely sacred in their frost, and urges them on me. Forty years ago, her young man, as gray and unaware as an English butterfly blinded by fog, fluttered amazed across this cerulean light, sagged, and exploded. I select two or three purple grapes, and one of them bursts inside my mouth. But they are not nearly enough for her to give, and she urges me on and on, till all she holds in her fingers is the hulled branch of the vine. It sways like a tree set on fire and thrown into water. She looks into the sky. It holds. All her offerings are gone.

May Morning

Deep into spring, winter is hanging on. Bitter and skillful in his hopelessness, he stays alive in every shady place, starving along the Mediterranean: angry to see the glittering sea-pale boulder alive with lizards green as Judas leaves. Winter is hanging on. He still believes. He tries to catch a lizard by the shoulder. One olive tree below Grottaglie welcomes the winter into noontime shade, and talks as softly as Pythagoras. Be still, be patient, I can hear him say, cradling in his arms the wounded head, letting the sunlight touch the savage face.

In Memory of Hubert Robert

A Hillside in Fiesole

An ancient city is the only place where the ancient creatures have room to become new. This wild rabbit has allowed her children to scamper among the tough green weeds near the ruins. Delicately fluffy and light as the parachutes of milkweed, the children would be young and ignorant in any case, so I let them go by. But she is the one I love to look on, she is the youthful one, in spite of the winter she has somehow got through. Her muscular hind legs are terrible weapons of defense and flight, but her forepaws in repose are gentle, as her long wiry whiskers flick precisely above them, branches ready for blossom in the green twilight.

POPPIES IN TRAJAN'S MARKET

For once among the centuries, it is not human blood, this scattering of a wild thing among the stones of a splendid human place. As far as I know, not even the emperor ordered men to be disposed of here, his friends, his enemies, or the strange kings of Africa too hopelessly proud to cut and bear stones on their shoulders or wrestle in the arena with starved orangutans or race the fleet ostriches in irregular circles. And today, for once, in Rome, a whole week has gone by, and I have not heard of a single recent murder. No. The brilliant scattering of scarlet petals here belongs in a field near the sea, and the stone belongs deep in a hill. Both stone and flower stand homeless beside each other here, strangers among the bewildering Romans.

The Cross

It is one of the longest afternoons of the world, an afternoon long past one of our wars. On the ruined wall of the mayor's house in Anghiari, some soldier, wandering up and down the city and exploring it, paused long enough to stitch a cross precisely with bullets. He must have done it for love of his art, for no Christ hangs there now. Somehow a seed from the field of wild dill blossoms paused in its own wandering and exploring flight, halfway up the mountain city, and I can see the solitary long stem and the golden crown, and the root in the crevice, the root also wandering and exploring the elegant cross on the wall stone, the machine-gunned cross. By this time the soldier is scattered farther away than the seed of the dill.

The Aristocrat

All over Apulia, currents of sea air snarl among winds from the landwise mountains. I can see thistle seeds tumbling everywhere, but I lose their pathways, they are so many. Flowers of every color flock up and down the walls of white ruin and beyond, between the snaggles of useless rock and the sea, poppies and camomilla clustered together like brilliant sheep. But somehow the thistle, disdainful in the general flight of seeds, ends up alone in the mob of wildflowers. Its bloom is so wealthy it would become scarlet, but scarlet is not the name. Scarlet is the shadow the poppies already wear. The thistle pauses all alone, elegant in its tatters, too proud to name itself, too aloof to accept any name I might give.

Epistle from the Amphitheatre

Dear, I have gone through a long slow summer and an autumn which is hard for me to understand. Italy is a new country, a country I never knew. Italy is so old. Here in Verona the Romans built an amphitheatre of pink marble nearly a thousand years before Amerigo Vespucci was born. Yet today the Arena stands still, nearly flawless. Its shape holds so fine a balance between the ground and the sky that its very stones are a meeting and an intermingling of light and shadow. At noon, even the fierce Italian sunlight cannot force a glare out of the amphitheatre's gentleness. In late twilight the Arena can hold twenty-two thousand people who still have plenty of room to hold their breath. If some person, welcome and yet alien to this place, is foolish enough to applaud the musicians in the Arena while they are still singing, some Veronese lover of the music will briefly, decisively hush up the stranger. The Veronese hush in defense of the music is a kind of indrawn breath. It sounds as though silence itself had spoken. And yet you can hear it from one end of the enormous Arena to the other, a clear whisper to the inner ear of the stranger: Shut up and listen. Be still. Be glorified. Or be damned.

Still, I wonder why it is hard for me to understand this Italian autumn. I think it is because the warmth has lasted so long. Verona is a city older than the Romans, and out of its old age it moved something in the sleep of those sparkling and victorious young engineers. I myself was once in an army, an excellent army as armies go, and I know it is almost immoral for a soldier to get out of bed in the morning until some barbaric Draco from West Virginia blasts him out of sleep with a whistle. Nick Bottom has nothing on me. I have a reasonably good ear for music, and when I am alone, I can hear voices that spoke to me twenty years ago more clearly than I can hear the oratorical squalls of Mario Proccacino. (Dear, you don't know his name. Never mind. It is enough for you to know that he is not a Veronese. He is not even an Italian. He is an American. An American statesman. He has a certain voice. His voice is a mistake; but it is unmistakable.) The young Roman soldiers who rose before daybreak in Verona were not moralists. They were pious men. The pious man, sang Virgil, does his duty with love. The restless young Roman legionaries stationed in Verona rose out of bed without being screamed at, and they found they had been given what in the American army today is still called good duty. Disciplined, intelligent young masters of roads and walls, those young Romans gazed full-face into their first daylight. Having slept dreamless, they dreamed by molding and lifting in place this new Arena, a comely body whose very stones give a new shape to the air that people breathe, hush, whisper, and listen to.

Those engineers were so young. Deep in the Alps, minerals hard enough to cut perfect diamonds had already been crumbling, a handful of grains every thousand years or so, and flowing downhill as the ice melted into the river Adige. And the young Romans woke beside the Adige.

Today, in the middle of my own life, I woke beside the Adige. We hurried through breakfast for once, because the sun was splendid, and we wanted to enter the Arena and to walk all the way around it. We climbed and stood as far away from each other as we could get without falling off the rim, as Amerigo Vespucci might have done. Far away I could see her, tiny and blazing in her golden skin, her wide-brimmed straw hat fluttering, one feather of one wing, still ascending. Instantly, we came home. I was impatient to write to you, because I do not want to waste time.

The Fox at Eype

He knows that all dogs bounding here and there, from the little vales all the way to the cliff-meadows and Thorncombe Beacon and beyond, are domestically forbidden to kill him. So every evening just before the end of twilight he emerges softly from the hedge across the lane and sits elegantly till darkness, gazing, with a certain weary amusement, into the middle distance of the sea.

A First Day in Paris

Some twenty years ago I was still a young man. I did not know anything more about Paris than a small black-haired sea tern knows about inland mountain gardens on the first day of his life. All he does is gaze around him, puzzled at the solitary distances of the ocean. How many mountains I have flown across, how many nests I have lain down in and abandoned between the big American cities. Now I walk in the gardens of the Tuileries. Here, a song tells me, some twenty years ago the chestnut buds in April were too heavy to bear themselves any longer. When a late frost fell on them, they suddenly shuddered in the night, and the next morning they opened, green as before, in spite of everything. The startled frost ran off and vanished, and the open blossoms turned white in their own good time. In Paris the natural world, alert and welcome in a moment to its own loveliness, offers a strange new face, as though God were creating it for the first time. Sometimes the women in the Tuileries grow so old they outlive death, and their shadows lie on chestnut leaves like sunlight.

The Sunlight Falling at Peace
in Moret-sur-Loing

At ten o'clock on this midsummer morning the wings of summer mosquitoes appear in the sunlight across the water. Sudden and brief, they flash into sight and out again. They move in the light, deep in its summer life, exposed and defenseless. I am too far away to glimpse their real bodies, but I know they are there because of the light they give. I remember a man long ago who could not bear to look on the face of God, and who fell to his knees in prayer at the sight of a beloved human face. The mosquitoes move again, deep in the light. They are like the blue veins that girls do their best to hide on the backs of their hands for fear somebody will catch their blood in the act and remind them that they too will grow old. But the obscene calamity of gray faces and cynical knowingness is a despair that the mosquitoes are likely to escape. The swallows resting under the stone bridge are waiting for twilight and its hungers, but the mosquitoes neither know nor care.

The river, the Loing, moves so lightly it seems adrift from its reeds. Fish nuzzle the surface into ripples that lie there a long time before they slide over to the marges. Two small boys chatter like finches and sway at the ends of their fishing poles. Their voices nuzzle the surface of the sky, and lie there a long time before they slide over to the roof of the church, lost finally in the voice of the old bell. The river, the Loing, moves so lightly it seems forever still. I would rather forget it is moving. I would rather forget that its fate guides it, with its small boys and fish and fishermen, downstream, to enter the dark red waters of the Marne.

Beside the Tour Magne in Nîmes

The tower is a long way up, and though I am no one to search out difficult valleyways to climb, I have strained up here freely, and now I have got what I came for. A breathing space. One thing I love about the stones here, even beyond their tottering and ramshackle balance, is their namelessness. Not even the doctors of history, with their fine hands sifting the skeletons of ancient leaves away from the branches of lost children's hands, can find on the great tower the slightest scar that can tell who built it here and left it for someone finally to approach and leave alone. Nearly every stone the Romans laid on it has long since rolled back down the hill. I am delighted to leave the tower alone, to lie down beside it on the high grass, feeling only a little less young and silly than a Roman, alive and at peace with the purposes of men's names I bless and will never know, names I will never have to be sorry that I knew.

Goodnight

By the Seine in the evening on the right-hand shore north of the Pont Alexandre, gangs of workmen have left a tangle of canvas and boards. A ditch opens there on the other side of the sycamores. I imagine by daylight the place must look like a wound. But the trees have been shedding their bark at the end of August, and their new skin, a peculiar golden, welcomes the lamplight thrown lightly from the ancient bridge, as well as whatever moonlight can find its way down the river. The trees might cling to the light forever, but they hold on for a moment only, and shed whatever lamplights and moons they have all over the torn ground, the lumber, the dirty canvas, and the four eyes of rats hurrying from the shadow beside the river to the strange new light on the other side of the trees. Soundless behind them, François Villon waves goodnight to his kinsmen.

Against Surrealism

There are some tiny obvious details in human life that survive the divine purpose of boring fools to death. In France, all the way down south in Avallon, people like to eat cake. The local bakers there spin up a little flour and chocolate into the shape of a penguin. We came back again and again to a certain window to admire a flock of them. But we never bought one.

We found ourselves wandering through Italy, homesick for penguins.

Then a terrible and savage fire of the dog-days roared all over the fourteenth arrondissement: which is to say, it was August: and three chocolate penguins appeared behind a window near Place Denfert-Rochereau. We were afraid the Parisians would recognize them, so we bought them all and snuck them home under cover.

We set them out on a small table above half the rooftops of Paris. I reached out to brush a tiny obvious particle of dust from the tip of a beak. Suddenly the dust dropped an inch and hovered there. Then it rose to the beak again.

It was a blue spider.

If I were a blue spider, I would certainly ride on a train all the way from Avallon to Paris, and I would set up my house on the nose of a chocolate penguin. It's just a matter of common sense.

Come, Look Quietly

The bird on the terrace has his own name in French, but I don't know it. He may be a nuthatch, only he doesn't eat upside down.

He has a perfectly round small purple cap on his crown and a slender long mask from his ears to his eyes all the way across. Come, look quietly. All the way across Paris. Far behind the bird, the globes of Sacré Coeur form out of the rain and fade again, all by themselves. The daylight all across the city is taking its own time.

The plump Parisian wild bird is scoring a light breakfast at the end of December. He has found the last seeds left in tiny cones on the outcast Christmas tree that blows on the terrace.

Afterword

Christopher Merrill

The Shape of Light is a pivotal book in James Wright's body of work—the bridge, in the words of his widow, Anne Wright, "which led from the dark of Ohio to the light of Italy and France." It is a bridge built of prose, which links the conflicting passions at the heart of his work—light and darkness, present and past, his native instincts and his growing cosmopolitanism; a kind of sketchbook in which the artist meticulously records what is in front of him, in sharp lines and tints. Memory was crucial to Wright's poetic practice, but on his European travels, particularly in 1973, and again in 1974, 1977 and 1979, he embarked on a different sort of journey, inward and outward, discovering new angles of vision, new ways of writing. The prose pieces that emerged from Wright's notebook, from his disciplined observation and new-found freedom from the verse line, illuminated his last two collections of poems, *To a Blossoming Pear Tree* and the posthumous *This Journey.*

There had been other bridges, notably poetry itself, which carried Wright from the constrictions of Depression-era childhood in Martins Ferry, Ohio, to the possibilities of a larger world—to Kenyon College, where he came under the tutelage of John Crowe Ransom; to the University of Washington, where he studied with Theodore Roethke and wrote a dissertation on Charles Dickens; to academic appointments, in Minneapolis and New York City, and complications in his private life (a failed marriage, alcoholism); to the Pulitzer Prize and the esteem of his fellow poets. What better vehicle of escape for a boy who grew up along the Ohio River? Wright knew more poems by heart than any American poet of his generation—and perhaps of any other.

Then there was the bridge forged from his translations of Neruda, Machado, and Trakl, which led to his breakthrough publication, in 1963, of *The Branch Will Not Break*, a crucial volume of poetry in modern American letters. But while the dramatic shift from the tightly controlled lyrics of his first two books, *The Green Wall* and *Saint Judas*, to the Deep Image poems of *The Branch Will Not Break* and *Shall We Gather at the River*, has been well documented, the role of *The Shape of Light* in his final poetic transformation is less known. "But I care more now for the poetry of the present moment," he writes in a poem about Catullus, as piccolini swim by him in a lake formed by volcanic activity. It is this letting go of the past that makes possible the light of his last poems. What he found in the present is what endures in his work long after his death, in 1980.

Many of the poems begin with the poet sitting in an outdoor café, observing his immediate surroundings. He opens his notebook and attends to what is there—a lizard, a spider, a turtle, a snail shell, trees, birds: almost anything can trigger his imagination, which inevitably veers into memory, speculation, improvisation, imperative. Every tone is registered in these paragraphs, from anger to grief, from bewilderment to love and praise. "Come, Look Quietly," the title of a poem about a "plump Parisian wild bird," might stand for Wright's method: he invites us to see what he sees, in all of its beauty.

And the world is filled with light, especially in Italy, the sunlit sanctuary of poets through the ages from northern latitudes. Like Keats and Goethe, Wright traveled south in search of another way of life, and what he found in the land of his beloved Horace and Catullus, in the realm of eternal verities, was a language informed by the speech rhythms of his native land and inflected through an array of literary traditions—a language adequate to the demands of the moment and destined to survive him: "Limone, wreath of the Garda mountains, the stone villa of Catullus still stands down at the far southern end of the lake. I hope you are in blossom when his ghost comes home."

Wright was a prolific letter writer, and *The Shape of Light* has epistolary qualities. Indeed his "Letter to Franz Wright" includes several paragraphs from a letter to his eldest son. (It is worth noting the differences between the letter collected in *A Wild Perfection: The Selected Letters of James Wright* and the poem. The paternal advice—not to leave school and bum around

Europe—is faintly ironic, since this is precisely what he was doing then, to good effect.) Three excerpts from letters to Donald Hall point to the evolution of his thought back of *The Shape of Light*: first, from Dorchester, Dorset, on June 26, 1973, when he was smarting from a bad review of his *Collected Poems*:

> We haven't been in touch for a very long time, Don, not really. I've been realizing lately that this is a hell of a note, because the truth is that I seem to be losing touch with myself, if you follow me. I don't mean I'm boozing (I'm not), or that I'm ill in any other way (the doc at home says I'm in good shape). I just seem to have lost touch with poetry and don't know quite where to turn. I feel low about it.

Two months later, from Venice, Wright sounds a different note:

> We have been having a divine summer of traveling and often loafing. For some reason, partly weariness and partly something else, I haven't been writing many poems. I do have a notebook which I keep pretty faithfully, and I found myself realizing the other day that I was having fun with it. It's been a long

time since I regarded writing as much fun, so
the notebook may mean something, even if I
don't know what [...]

And a month after that, from Vienna, he asks Hall to give his
regards to the British poet Geoffrey Hill, whose latest book,
Mercian Hymns, has captivated him:

I found the book in London last summer,
and by this time I must have read it at least
twenty times. I wrote a good many notes on
it in my notebook, and one of these days I
may even try to write an essay about it. It is
wonderfully original, and it also suggests
further lines of development, the first poly-
semous book of that kind that I've seen in a
good while.

Hill's sequence of thirty prose meditations on the life of
King Offa, who reigned over the greater part of England in
the second half of the eighth century, may at first glance
seem far removed from Wright's project. But *The Shape of Light*
can also be read on many levels. And the prose rhythms that
Wright explores, the lines of development that he follows to
their natural limits, continue to invigorate American poetry.

In a meditation on Venice, Wright discovered a new route
from hell to heaven, poetically speaking: "It is only the
evenings that give the city the shape of light; they make the

darkness frail and they give substance to the light." Still in his early forties, he could not know that he had already entered the evening of his life. But this was when he learned how to give substance to the light within, balancing the anger that he felt toward his own country and its debased politics—"the final place, New York, America, hell on earth"—with what he finds near to hand. Thus the bombing in Cambodia receives but passing reference in a poem set on the shore of Lake Garda, on the Feast of the Assumption; his contempt for Richard Nixon is leavened with sardonic humor: "I lay you eight to five that you will go blind if you take a walk at high noon with the President of the United States. I love my country for its light." In fact he seeks a different light, a European light drenched in history and poetry—the light of transcendence, which appears in the final lines of *This Journey*: "Now we are all sitting here strangely/ On top of the sunlight." The route from the visible to the invisible was what James Wright sketched out in *The Shape of Light*. In the things of the earth, the vagaries of his heart, and the history of a botched civilization, he glimpsed another realm, permanent and holy, and wrote his way toward that light.

—Christopher Merrill

Volume 3
10,000 Dawns: The Love Poems of Claire and Yvan Goll
Translated by Thomas Rain Crowe and Nan Watkins
1-893996-27-1   88 pages $14.00

Volume 2
There Is No Road: Proverbs by Antonio Machado
Translated by Mary G. Berg & Dennis Maloney
1-893996-66-2   118 pages $14.00

Volume I
Wild Ways: Zen Poems of Ikkyu
Translated by John Stevens
1-893996-65-4   152 pages $14.00